Lounge

Sing Along with 8 Great-Sounding

G000153682

Contents

Alfred Publishing Co., Inc.
16320 Roscoe Blvd., Suite 100
P.O. Box 10003
Van Nuys, CA 91410-0003
alfred.com

ISBN-10: 0-7390-4447-8 (Book and CD)
ISBN-13: 978-0-7390-4447-6 (Book and CD)

Cover Art:
Musicians: © DigitalVision®, Ltd.
Microphone: © istockphoto.com/picpics

Come Fly with Me

Lyric by
SAMMY CAHN
Music by
JAMES VAN HEUSEN

Come fly with me!
Let's fly, let's fly away.
If you can use
some exotic booze,
there's a bar in far Bombay.
Come fly with me.
Let's fly, let's fly away.

Come fly with me!
Let's float down to Peru!
In Llama Land
there's a one-man band,
and he'll toot
his flute for you.
Come fly with me.
Let's take off in the blue!
Once I get you up there,
where the air is rarified,
we'll just glide,
starry-eyed.
Once I get you up there,
I'll be holding you so near,
you may hear
the angels cheer,
because we're together.

Weather-wise,
it's such a lovely day!
Just say the words
and we'll beat those birds
down to Acapulco Bay.
It's perfect
for a flying honeymoon, they say.
So, come fly with me.
Let's fly, let's fly away.
Oh, come on and fly!

(Inst. solo)

Once I get you up there,
where the air is rarified,
we'll just glide,
starry-eyed.
Once I get you up there,
I'll be holding you so near,
you may the hear
all the angels cheer,
because we're together.

Weather-wise,
it's such a lovely day!
You just say those words
and we'll beat those birds
down to Acapulco Bay.
It's so perfect
for a flying honeymoon, they say.
Come fly with me,
let's fly, let's fly.
Pack up, let's fly away!

Come Fly with Me

Lyric by
SAMMY CAHN

Music by
JAMES VAN HEUSEN

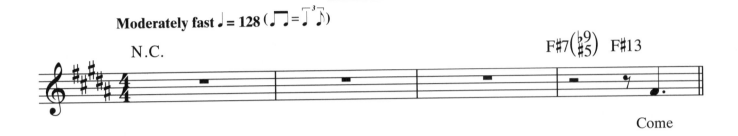

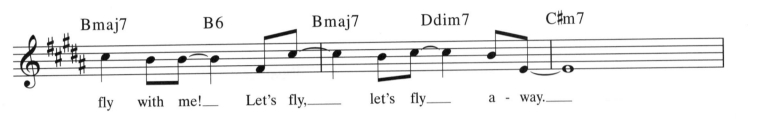

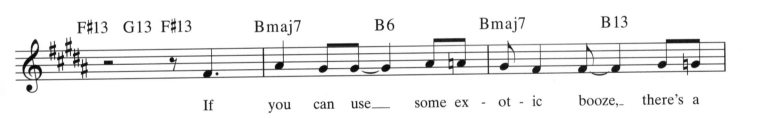

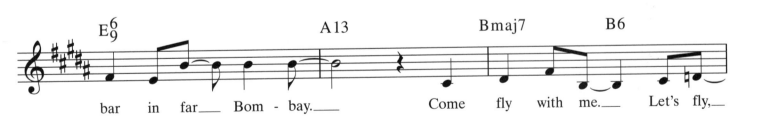

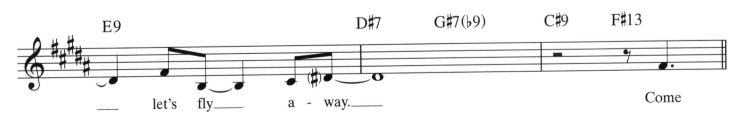

Come Fly With Me - 4 - 1
26508

4

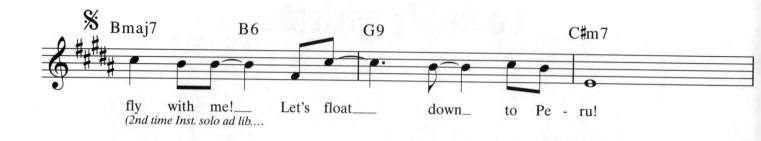

fly with me!__ Let's float__ down_ to Pe - ru!
(2nd time Inst. solo ad lib....

In Lla - ma Land_ there's a one-man band,_ and he'll

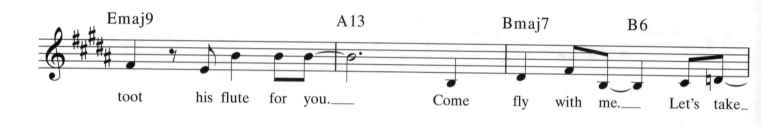

toot his flute for you.__ Come fly with me.__ Let's take_

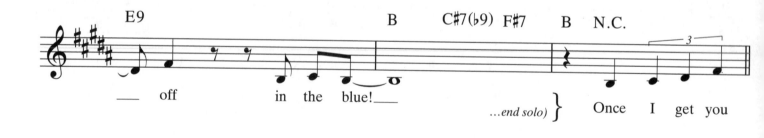

__ off in the blue!__ *...end solo)* Once I get you

up there, where the air is rar - i - fied,__

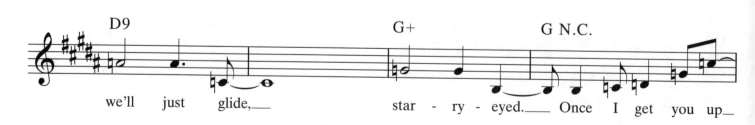

we'll just glide,__ star - ry - eyed.__ Once I get you up_

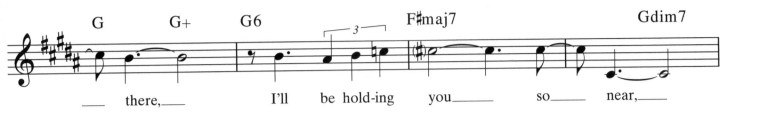

there,___ I'll be hold-ing you___ so___ near,___

you may hear {the all the} an - gels cheer, be - cause we're to-geth-er.

Weath-er - wise,___ it's such___ a love - ly day!___

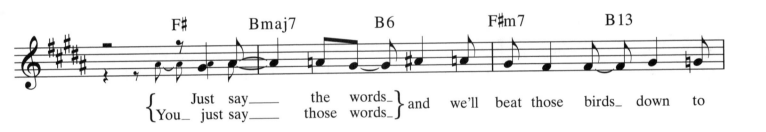

{Just say___ the words__} {You__ just say___ those words__} and we'll beat those birds_ down to

A - ca-pul - co Bay.___ It's per - fect for a fly -

ing___ hon - ey - moon,___ they say.___ So, come

6

fly   with   me.___   Let's   fly,___   let's   fly   a - way.___

Oh,   come on and fly!

___   It's   so

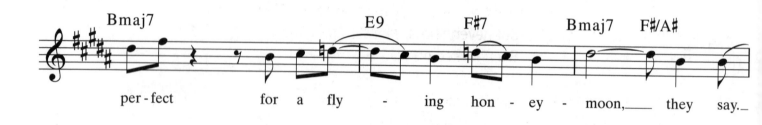

per - fect   for   a   fly   -   ing   hon - ey - moon,___   they   say.___

___   Come   fly___   with   me,___   let's   fly,___   let's   fly.___

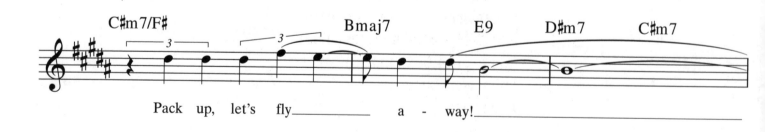

Pack   up,   let's   fly___   a - way!___

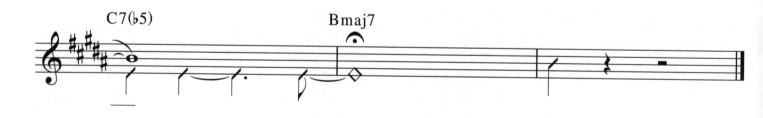

Don't Get Around Much Anymore

Lyric by
BOB RUSSELL
Music by
DUKE ELLINGTON

Missed the Saturday dance,
heard they crowded the floor.
Couldn't bear it without you,
don't get around much anymore.
Thought I'd visit the club,
got as far as the door.
They'd have asked me about you,
don't get around much anymore.

Darling, I guess my mind's more at ease.
But nevertheless, why stir up memories?
Been invited on dates,
might have gone but what for?
Awf'lly diff'rent without you,
don't get around much anymore.

(Inst. solo)

Darlin', I guess, my mind's more at ease.
But nevertheless, why stir up memories?
Whoa, been invited on dates.
Might have gone, but what for?
Oh, it's diff'rent without you,
I can't bear it without you, darlin', no.
Please, girl, oh, I need you, baby.
Don't get around much anymore.
I don't get around much anymore.
I need you, baby.
I need you, baby.

Don't Get Around Much Anymore

Lyric by
BOB RUSSELL

Music by
DUKE ELLINGTON

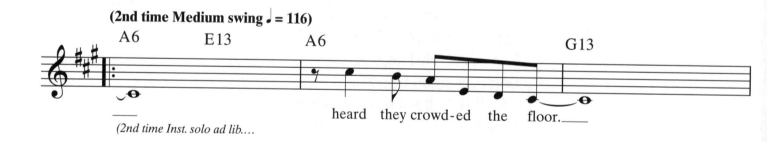

*F𝄪 = G♮

Don't Get Around Much Anymore - 4 - 1
26508

you,___ don't get a-round much an-y-more.

Faster

...end solo)

Dar - lin', I guess, my mind's___ more at

ease.___ But nev - er - the - less,___ why___

___ stir up mem - o - ries?___ Whoa,___ been_ in -

vit - ed on dates._ Might have gone, but what for?___ Oh, it's

I Get a Kick Out of You

Words and Music by
COLE PORTER

I get no kick from champagne.
Mere alcohol doesn't thrill me at all.
So tell me why should it be true
that I get a kick out of you?

Some, they may go for cocaine.
I'm sure that if I took even one sniff,
it would bore me terrific'lly too.
Yet I get a kick out of you.

I get a kick ev'ry time
I see you standing there before me.
I get a kick tho' it's clear to see
you obviously do not adore me.

I get no kick in a plane.
Flying too high with some gal in the sky
is my idea of nothing to do.
Yet I get a kick,
mm, you give me a boot.
I get a kick out of you.

I Get a Kick Out of You

Words and Music by
COLE PORTER

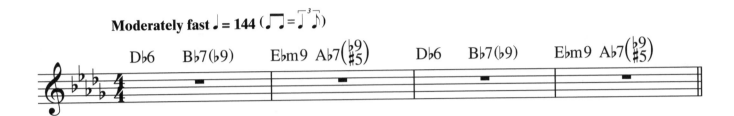

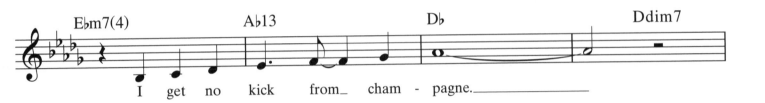

I get no kick from champagne.

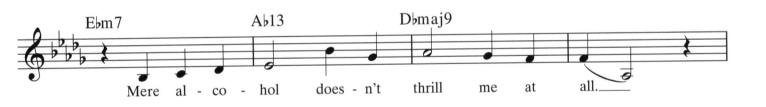

Mere al-co-hol does-n't thrill me at all.

So tell me why should it be true that

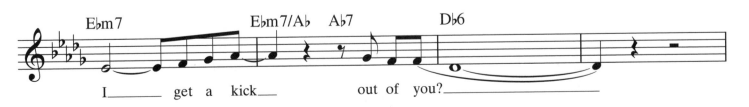

I get a kick out of you?

I Get a Kick Out of You - 3 - 1
26508

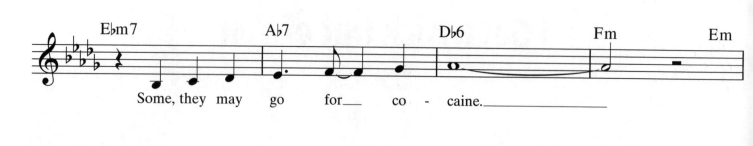

Some, they may go for___ co - caine._____

I'm sure that if I took e - ven___ one sniff, it would

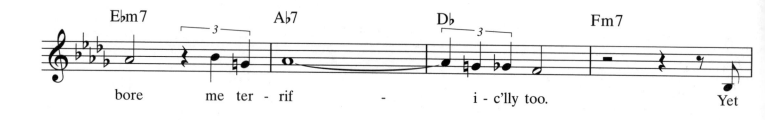

bore me ter - rif - i - c'lly too. Yet

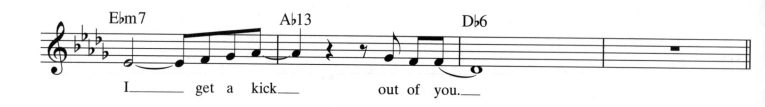

I_____ get a kick___ out of you.___

I_____ get a kick___ ev - 'ry time_____ I see you

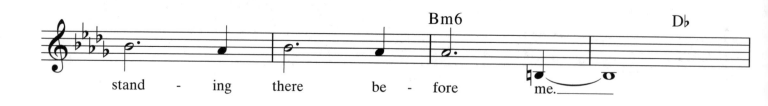

stand - ing there be - fore me.___

I get a kick tho' it's clear to see you

I've Got You Under My Skin

Words and Music by
COLE PORTER

I've got you under my skin.
I've got you deep in the heart of me.
So deep in my heart
that you're really a part of me.
I've got you under my skin.

I tried so not to give in.
I said to myself,
"This affair never will go so well."
But why should I try to resist,
when, baby, I know so well?
I've got you under my skin.

I'd sacrifice anything,
come what might,
for the sake of having you near.
In spite of a warning voice
that comes in the night and repeats,
repeats in my ear,
"Don't you know, little fool,
you never can win?
Use your mentality.
Wake up to reality."
But each time that I do,
just the thought of you
makes me stop before I begin,
'cause I've got you under my skin.

(Inst. solo)

I would sacrifice anything,
come what might,
for the sake of having you near.
In spite of a warning voice
that comes in the night and repeats,
how it yells in my ear,
"Don't you know, little fool,
you never can win?
Why not use your mentality?
Step up, wake up to reality."
But each time I do,
just the thought of you
makes me stop just before I begin
'cause I've got you under my skin.
Yes, I've got you under my skin.

I've Got You Under My Skin

Words and Music by
COLE PORTER

I've Got You Under My Skin - 4 - 1
26508

tried so_____ not__ to give in._____ I

(2nd time Inst. solo ad lib....

said to my - self,__ "This af - fair__ nev-er will go___ so well."_____ But

why should I try__ to re - sist,___ when, ba - by, I know__ so well?_____

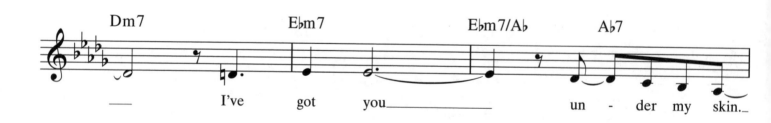

—— I've got you_____ un - der my skin._

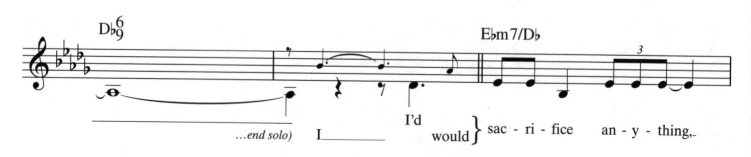

_____ *...end solo)* I_____ I'd would } sac - ri - fice an - y - thing,_

come what might,_ for the sake__ of hav-ing you near._ In spite of a warn-

ing voice__ that comes in the night__ and re - peats,_

re - peats in my ear,__ "Don't you know,_ lit - tle fool,_____
how it yells_ in my ear,__ "Don't you know, lit - tle fool,_____

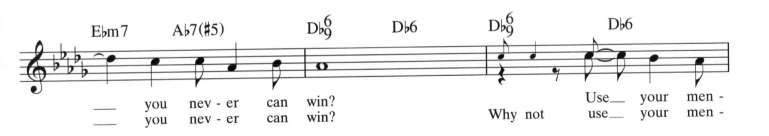

____ you nev - er can win?

____ you nev - er can win? Why not

Use__ your men -
use__ your men -

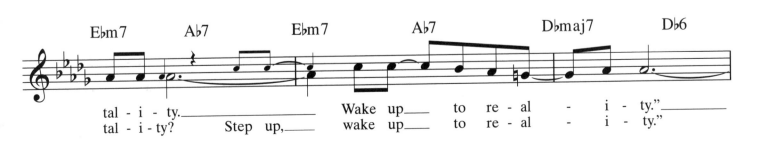

tal - i - ty._____ Wake up__ to re - al - i - ty."___
tal - i - ty? Step up,___ wake up__ to re - al - i - ty."

But each time___ that I do,___ just the thought

But___ each time I do,___ just the thought

of you___ makes me stop be-fore I be-gin,___

of you___ makes me stop just be-fore I be-gin,___ 'cause I've

got you___ un-der my skin.

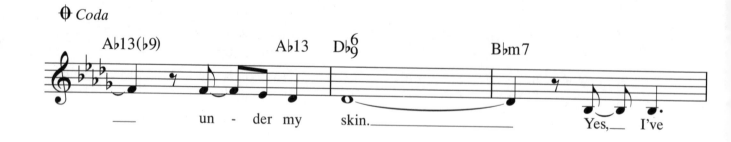

un-der my skin.___ Yes,___ I've

got you___ un-der my skin.

Just a Gigolo

Words and Music by
IRVING CAESAR, JULIUS BRAMMER and LEONELLO CASUCCI

I'm just a gigolo, and ev'rywhere I go,
people know the part I'm playing.
Paid for ev'ry dance, selling each romance,
ooh, what they're sayin'.
There will come a day when youth will pass away.
What will they say about me?
When the end comes, I know
I was just a gigolo.
Life goes on without me.

I'm just a gigolo, and ev'rywhere I go,
people know the part I'm playing.
Paid for ev'ry dance, selling each romance,
ooh, what they're sayin'.
There will come a day when youth will pass away.
What will they say about me?
When the end comes, I know
I was just a gigolo.
Life goes on without me.

'Cause, I ain't got nobody.
Nobody cares for me,
nobody, nobody cares for me,
I'm so sad and lonely,
sad and lonely, sad and lonely.
Won't some sweet mama
come and take a chance with me,
'cause I ain't so bad.
Been alone, baby,
been sad and lonesome all of the time.
Even on the beat,
on and on and on the beat.
Bop. Boyzee, boyzee bop. Ditty bop.

I ain't got nobody.
Nobody cares for me, nobody, nobody.
Hey! Say! See it, man got soul, *whoa!*
See, I'm all alone. Baby, get it?
Anybody got it?
A little soul, little love soul.
Ah! Hoo!

Ain't got nobody, hoo!
This a love song. Need a love.
Omily, babily, zimily, babily,
omily, babily, zimily bop.

I ain't got nobody.
Nobody, nobody cares for me.
Nobody cares for me.
I'm so sad and lonely,
sad and lonely, sad and lonely.
Won't some sweet mama
come and take a chance with me,
'cause I ain't so bad.
Keep up that soul.
Play a love song all of the time.
Even on the beat,
on and on and on the beat.
Get it low, Joe, jolly, mama, baby,
still got nobody, not love.
Say it now. Nobody. Nobody.

Nobody. Nobody.
No one. No one.
Lutilu. Got it, got it.
Get it, get it.
Gotta see the one over there.
Nobody.
Got no one.
Nobody. Nobody.
Nobody. Nobody.
Nobody cares for me.

Just a Gigolo

Words and Music by
IRVING CAESAR, JULIUS BRAMMER
and LEONELLO CASUCCI

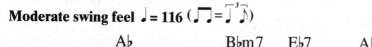

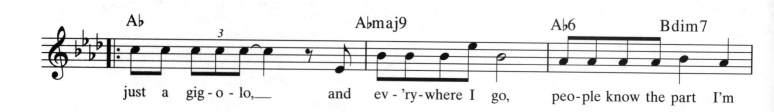

just a gig-o-lo,___ and ev-'ry-where I go, peo-ple know the part I'm

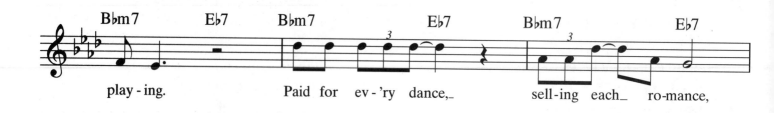

play-ing. Paid for ev-'ry dance,_ sell-ing each_ ro-mance,

ooh, what they're say-in'._____ There will come a day_ when

youth will pass a-way. What will they say a-bout me? When the

Just a Gigolo - 5 - 1
26508

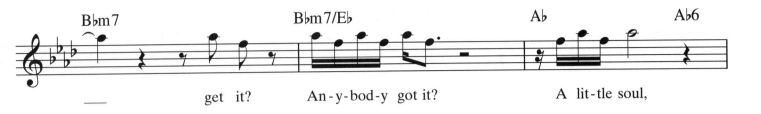

get it? An-y-bod-y got it? A lit-tle soul,

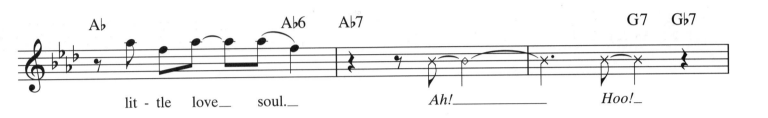

lit - tle love_ soul._ *Ah!*_ *Hoo!*_

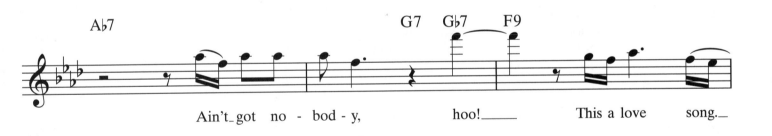

Ain't_ got no - bod - y, hoo!_ This a love song._

Need a love.

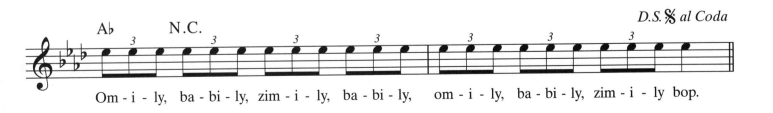

D.S. %% al Coda

Om - i - ly, ba - bi - ly, zim - i - ly, ba - bi - ly, om - i - ly, ba - bi - ly, zim - i - ly bop.

Just a Gigolo - 5 - 4
26508

26

The Lady Is a Tramp

Words by
LORENZ HART
Music by
RICHARD RODGERS

She gets too hungry
for dinner at eight.
She likes the theater,
but never comes late.
She never bothers
with people she'd hate.
That's why the lady is a tramp.

Doesn't like crap games
with Barons or Earls,
won't go to Harlem
in ermine and pearls,
won't dish the dirt
with the rest of the girls.
That's why the lady is a tramp.

She likes the free,
fresh wind in her hair,
life without care.
She's broke, and it's oke.
Hates California,
it's cold and it's damp.
That's why the lady is a tramp.

She gets too hungry
to wait for for dinner at eight.
She likes the theater,
but never comes late.
She'd never bother
with people she'd hate.
That's why the lady is a tramp.

She'll have no crap games,
with sharpies and frauds,
and she won't go to Harlem,
in Lincolns or Fords,
and she won't dish the dirt
with the rest of them broads.
That's why the lady is a tramp.

She loves the free,
fresh wind in her hair,
life without care.
She's broke, but it's oke.
Hates California,
it's so cold and so damp.
That's why the lady,
that's why the lady,
that's why the lady is a tramp.